The Spring Cup

Christian Holzmann

HELBLING LANGUAGES

www.helblinglanguages.com

The Spring Cup
by Christian Holzmann
© HELBLING LANGUAGES 2007

First published 2007
Reprinted 2009

ISBN 978-3-85272-005-0

The publishers would like to thank the following for their kind permission to reproduce the following photographs and other copyright material: Alamy p6, p30, p31.

Series editor Maria Cleary
Illustrated by Francesca Galmozzi
Activities by Elspeth Rawstron
Design and layout by Capolinea
Printed by Athesia

About this Book

Level 3 Structures

Present continuous for future	Cardinal / ordinal numbers
Present perfect	*One / ones*
Present perfect versus past simple	Reflexive pronouns
Should / shouldn't (advice and obligation)	Indefinite pronouns
Must / should	
Need to / have to	*Too* plus adjective
Will	*Not* plus adjective plus enough
	Relative pronouns *who, which* and *that*
Ever / never	Prepositions of time, place and movement
Would like	
So do I / neither do I	
Question tags	

Structures from lower levels are also included

Contents

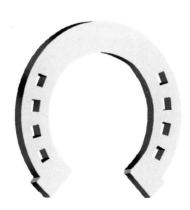

Before Reading

1 **Listen, to the text about the famous British horse rider, Ellen Whitaker and tick the correct words to complete the sentences below.**

a) Ellen Whitaker is one of the .... riders to represent Great Britain.
  1 ☐ tallest   **2** ☐ youngest   **3** ☐ oldest

b) She was born in Yorkshire in the .... of England.
  1 ☐ north   **2** ☐ south   **3** ☐ east

c) Two of her .... are famous horse riders.
  1 ☐ friends   **2** ☐ uncles   **3** ☐ brothers

d) She began riding before she could ....
  1 ☐ talk   **2** ☐ stand   **3** ☐ walk

e) The legal age to compete internationally is ....
  1 ☐ fourteen   **2** ☐ sixteen   **3** ☐ fifteen

2 **Now fill in the fact file about Ellen Whitaker.**

Name: ....

Age: ....

Nationality: ....

Appearance: ....

Profession: ....

3 **Write a fact file about your favourite sports personality.**

4 Match the characters from the story with the descriptions.

a)

b)

c)

d)

1 ☐ Hi! My name's Caroline. I've got long auburn hair. I love horses and I've got my own horse. I haven't won any competitions yet but I hope I will soon!

2 ☐ Hello. My name's Applewind. I'm Caroline's horse. I'm white and I've got a long tail and mane which Caroline brushes every day. I like show jumping and we enter a lot of competitions together but unfortunately we never win.

3 ☐ Hi! My name's Fred. I'm Caroline's brother. I've got short auburn hair. By the way, I haven't got a horse. In fact, I don't know anything about horses!

4 ☐ Hello, I'm Mr Morley and I'm the head of the stables. I've got grey hair and I'm going bald!

5 Look at the pictures in the book and guess the answers to these questions.

a) Who or what is Blossom?

b) Why does Sophie's horse fall?

c) Do you think the story will have a happy ending?

"Do you think you can win this competition, Caroline?" Mrs Winterbottom asked her daughter.

"I don't know, mum. But I'll do my best."

"I know, my dear. Just remember that your father pays a lot of money for the horse. And a lot of money for the stables˚. And a lot of money for the riding˚ club."

"I know, mum, I know. I'll do my best. I really will."

Caroline always did her best, but it was never enough. She was a good rider, and her horse Applewind was a great horse. She went to Sunshine Stables to ride Applewind. And she never missed˚ a competition. But Sophie Craig was always better than her. Sophie won all of the show jumping˚ competitions, and Sophie's horse Blossom was everybody's darling˚. Everyone loved Sophie and Blossom.

Glossary

- **darling:** (here) favourite
- **missed:** (here) didn't go to
- **riding:** (here) horse riding

- **show jumping:** sport where horses and riders jump over small walls and fences
- **stables:** place where you keep horses

"If you really want to win, you will win," Caroline's dad said. He said the same thing before every competition. "It's the same with my work. I want to win, so I win. Life is about winning. You have to learn that, Caroline!"

Caroline sighed°. "Dad," she said. "I want to win, too. But Sophie is too good."

"You have to be better than her," Mr Winterbottom said. "If you don't win, Caroline, I'll sell your horse. No trophy°, no horse! When is the next competition?"

"In five days, dad," Caroline said.

"I want you to win it, Caroline. If you win the competition, you can keep Applewind!"

Glossary

- **sighed:** took a long deep breath
- **trophy:** cup you win in a competition

What's the matter°, sis°?" It was Fred, Caroline's brother.
"Applewind again?"
"It's not Applewind, it's me," Caroline said. "Dad said that he'll sell Applewind if I don't win the next competition. But Sophie Craig always wins. She's too good. What can I do?"
Fred was sorry for his sister. He wanted to help her. But how? Caroline was right, Sophie was good. And Blossom was a great horse. Caroline worked hard, but Sophie also worked hard. Fred didn't know what to do. He sat down in his favourite armchair° and fell asleep. Suddenly he woke up with a jump.
"Sleep! That's the answer. Dad's sleeping pills°!"
He went to the bathroom. A minute later he had five sleeping pills in his hand.

- **armchair:** big comfortable chair with armrests
- **sis:** (abbrev.) sister

- **sleeping pills:** tablets (medicine) to make you sleep
- **what's the matter?:** what's the problem?

It was the day of the competition. "Hello, Sophie," smiled Mr Morley, the head of Sunshine Stables.

"The winner today qualifies° for an international competition."

"I know, sir. That would be great!"

"Good luck then, Sophie."

"Thank you, sir."

"Did you hear that, Blossom?" Sophie whispered into Blossom's ear. "We must win the competition today. Let's go and get ready!"

Sophie went to her box°. Fred was there. "Hi Fred," she said. "How's Caroline?" Fred said something she didn't understand and ran away.

"How strange!" Sophie thought. Then she gave Blossom a drink of water and got her ready for the competition.

"I'm so nervous," Caroline said to her brother.

"Don't worry," said Fred, "you'll win this time."

"Fred, I never win, I always come second!"

"Be more confident°," said Fred. "Hey, good luck, sis!"

Caroline looked at her watch. There were just ten minutes before the competition started. She saw Sophie and Blossom. Blossom's head was hanging down° and she looked a bit tired. But Caroline knew that Blossom was a great horse. Tired or not, Blossom was going to win again. And then her dad would sell Applewind. Caroline wanted to cry, but she had to be brave.

Glossary

- **box:** space for a horse inside a big stable
- **confident:** sure of your ability
- **hanging down:** bent; not up/straight
- **qualifies:** when you qualify for something, you pass a test that allows you to take part in it

The competition started. Blossom was first. She cleared° the first obstacle° easily. "Good! Great jump!" Sophie thought. She whispered into Blossom's ear: "Good girl! Go for it°." Blossom went on. There was a change of direction and then a double combination°. Sophie heard shouts of "Go, Blossom, go!" She felt great. "Spring Cup," she said out loud, "Spring Cup, here I come." There was a sharp° turn, then two wide jumps. Blossom was flying, and Sophie felt really good. "I'm flying," she thought. "I'm flying, but Blossom's not flying with me. Where is Blossom?" Then everything went black.

Glossary

- **cleared:** jumped over
- **double combination:** two jumps together
- **go for it:** do your best
- **obstacle:** fence or wall
- **sharp:** (here) sudden

Caroline was next. She knew something was wrong. People were shouting, but she had to go – first obstacle, change of direction, a combination and then another fence. "We're doing fine," she thought. "But what about time? Oh no! We're too slow!! Goodbye Applewind." She felt tears in her eyes. "My dad will sell Applewind, and I'll never see him again. Oh why, oh why, can't I win one competition – just one competition? Then I can keep my horse. And mum and dad will love me and be proud* of me for once."

• **proud:** pleased with someone

But what was that? From the corner of her eye she saw Blossom and Sophie. Sophie was holding her arm. She was all dirty, and there were lots of people standing around her. Then Caroline did another turn and cleared another fence. Yes!!!

A few moments later she finished the round. She looked up at the scoreboard°! She was first! She was the winner at last!

"And the winner is – Caroline on Applewind!"

Caroline was crying. Not because she was sad, but because she was happy.

"And the Spring Cup goes to Caroline Winterbottom on Applewind," Mr Morley said, as he handed her the big gold trophy.

"Well done, Caroline."

"Thank you, sir," she said. And then she asked. "What about Sophie? Is she alright? What happened?"

"We think that Blossom is sick. Sophie had a bad fall but she was lucky. She broke a rib°, but that's all. We don't know about Blossom. Her left leg doesn't look good."

"Oh, I'm so sorry for Sophie," Caroline said. "But I'm also happy that I won."

"You see," Mr Winterbottom shouted. "What did I say? If you want to win, you'll win. I'm so proud of you, darling. You're my champion."

"Thank you, dad," said Caroline. "Can I keep Applewind?"

"Of course, you can," Mr Winterbottom said. "But make sure° you win the next competition, too."

Glossary

- **make sure:** be certain to
- **rib:** one of the curved bones that go around your chest and back

- **scoreboard:** table that shows the position of the competitors

"What did I say?" Fred said to his sister. "I knew that you were going to win this time!" "I'm so happy," said Caroline, "but I only won because Blossom was sick. And as soon as Blossom gets better, I'll be coming second place again."

"Maybe Blossom will be sick again," Fred said. "What do you mean?" asked Caroline. "Blossom is never sick."

Fred looked embarrassed°. "Well, with a little help she can be sick..."

"Fred, what are you talking about?" Caroline shouted. "Do you know what happened to Blossom? Tell me right away°, Fred."

"Forget it," Fred said. "Be happy! You're the champion now! And dad won't sell your horse."

"Fred," Caroline said. "I need to talk to you. What did you mean when you said: 'with a little help Blossom can be sick'?"

Fred told Caroline about Blossom and the sleeping pills.

"Look, I'm sorry about Sophie and all that*, but I did it for you."

"Oh Fred!" Caroline cried. "Do you think I want to win like that? Do you really think that?"

"But I only wanted to help you. Look! Everyone is happy. You are, mum and dad are, Applewind is happy too, I think – and Sophie and Blossom will be okay in a few weeks."

"Fred! Sophie was lucky that she only broke a rib. Thank goodness she didn't break more. Thank goodness she's not dead!!"

Fred started crying. "I'm sorry, I'm really sorry. I didn't think... "

"That's alright, Fred," Caroline said, "I know you did it for me. But we have to tell everyone the truth. I don't want the Cup. Not like this!"

• **all that:** (here) everything else

"Wait!" Fred said. "Don't say anything. Sophie and Blossom will be alright. Everyone will be unhappy if you tell the truth. I won't do it again, I promise. But please don't say anything. You are the champion, Caroline. Everyone is happy and proud of you."

"I know," Caroline said, "but Sophie's not happy. And her parents aren't happy, either. And I'm not proud of winning the Cup like this."

"But Caroline, if you tell the truth, dad will sell Applewind."

"I know," said Caroline. And then she started crying.

The next day at the stables Caroline talked to Mr Morley.

"So you see, sir, I didn't win because I was the best. I won because of the sleeping pills. I'm very sorry, sir. I didn't know anything about it. And my brother is very sorry, too. He did it to help me. And he'll never do it again. But I can't accept° the Cup. I don't want to win the Cup like this."

"This is a very serious matter°," said Mr Morley. "You know Fred committed a crime°. If Sophie's parents go to the police your brother will be in real trouble°. Thank you for telling me, Caroline. I'll have to talk to your and Sophie's parents and decide what to do. I know it's not your fault but I may have to ask you to leave the stables."

"I know," Caroline said and she started to cry. "I'm sorry, too."

Glossary

- **accept:** take
- **be in real trouble:** have big problems
- **committed a crime:** did something that is against the law
- **matter:** situation

"My son's a criminal°. My daughter's not a champion! What will people say?" Mr Winterbottom shouted.

"I know, sir," said Mr Morley, "It doesn't look good. Maybe we can talk to Sophie's parents. Maybe we won't have to call the police. And maybe you can talk to your children and be nice to them."

"Nice? Nice? I give them everything they want. I'm nice enough."

"Mr Winterbottom," said Mr Morley seriously. "Getting things or winning isn't really important. Being happy is important."

Caroline's dad was silent. He knew that Mr Morley was right.

"Show Caroline that you love her for who she is, not for what she can do. Now, I'll talk to Mr and Mrs Craig and tell them you're sorry."

"Thanks," said Caroline's dad. "Can Caroline stay in the club?"

"I don't know. Let's see what Sophie's parents say."

Glossary

- **criminal:** someone who does something that is against the law

22

"Don't worry," said Sophie. "It wasn't your fault°. I'll be back riding° in a few weeks." "And Blossom?" asked Caroline.

"Blossom was lucky, too. She'll be able to jump again."

"I'm so sorry, Sophie. Fred did it for me. He meant well, he didn't think about the consequences°. My dad said he was going to sell Applewind. You know my dad. It's always winning, winning, winning."

"I know. Well, maybe you'll win the next competition," Sophie said.

"I don't think so," Caroline said. "Mr Morley won't want me in the stables now.

"I talked to Mr Morley," Sophie said. "And my parents talked to him, too. You don't need to leave. He said he wants to talk to Fred, too. I think he wants him to help out at the stables for a while so he'll understand more about horses."

"Sophie! Really! Why are you doing this for me?"

"Well," Sophie said, "you're a good rider. And I want to win against good riders, not bad riders." And she grinned°.

- **consequences:** results of an action
- **grinned:** gave a wide smile
- **I'll be back riding:** I'll be riding again
- **it wasn't your fault:** you didn't cause it

The morning was cold but sunny. Caroline and Sophie were exercising their horses. Blossom was okay again, and Applewind looked good, too.

"Come back, girls," Mr Morley shouted. "Time to clean the stables."

The girls sighed. How boring. "You know what?" said Sophie.

"Yes, I know," said Caroline and grinned.

"Let Fred muck out the stables and we'll go for another ride!" Sophie said.

"Race you to the woods," Caroline shouted. "And this time I'll beat you."

Mr Morley saw the girls on their horses, racing to the woods. He couldn't tell who was faster.

After Reading

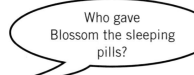

1 Talk about the story. Ask and answer questions using the words below.

sleeping pills	a lot of money	win	competition
sell	sick	a bad fall	in real trouble
help	broke a rib	leave the stables	

> Who gave Blossom the sleeping pills?

> Fred gave Blossom the sleeping pills.

2 Complete the sentences with the adjectives below.

tired	nervous	confident	lucky	happy

a) Sophie was .... before the show jumping competition.
b) Caroline was .... before the competition.
c) Blossom looked .... before the competition.
d) Caroline was .... when she won the competition.
e) Sophie was .... because she only broke a rib.

3 Now make sentences about the story with the adjectives and nouns below.

Example:
Sophie is a good rider.

Nouns	**Adjectives**
rider	bad
horse	expensive
fall	great
trophy	good
stables	gold

4 **Read the text about learning to ride and complete the sentences with the verbs below.**

fall off	look	find	take up
watch	have	feel	buy

So you want to (a) ……….. horse riding as a hobby? Remember riding can be a dangerous sport. A lot of people (b) ……….. accidents. You could (c) ……….. your horse. Or worse – you could get squashed, kicked or bitten by your horse.

So you still want to try horse riding? Well, first you need to (d) ……….. a good riding school and learn from a qualified instructor. You need to (e) ……….. happy and safe with your instructor and the school. You should visit some local riding schools and ask if you can (f) ……….. some beginner level lessons. The horses should (g) ……….. well cared for and the stables should be clean and tidy.

And remember, riding equipment is very expensive. Don't (h) ……….. everything before you start.You should have a few lessons first and see if you enjoy it. Then you can buy the hat, the boots, the jacket and the jodhpurs.

 5 **Now listen and check your answers.**

6 **In pairs, ask and answer questions about your hobbies.**

What is your hobby?
When did you start it?
What equipment do you need?
Why do you enjoy it?
How often do you do it?

After Reading

1 Read Caroline's diary entry and choose the correct word for each space.

Last week, there was a big show jumping (a) .... *which I wanted to win. My dad wanted me to win it too!! Well, as you know, I* (b) .... *a show jumping competition before.*

Sophie usually wins and I usually come second. Thanks to a little help from my brother, this competition was (c) .... *Yes, I won but I wasn't happy about it. Nobody was happy about it! Before the competition, Fred gave Sophie's horse Blossom some* (d) ....

Blossom fell asleep during the competition and Sophie (e) .... *and broke a rib. It was lucky she didn't die! And it was all my fault – well not all my fault – more my brother's fault.*

I told Mr Morley (f) .... *He told my parents and of course my father was very* (g) .... *Luckily Sophie and her parents were very nice about it all. Sophie didn't want me to leave the riding stables. She likes competing* (h) .... *me. So luckily, this story's got a happy ending.*

(a)	**1** competition	**2** obstacle	**3** champion
(b)	**1** never won	**2** have never win	**3** have never won
(c)	**1** different	**2** new	**3** the same
(d)	**1** sugar lumps	**2** sleeping pills	**3** sleepers
(e)	**1** was falling	**2** has fallen	**3** fell
(f)	**1** everything	**2** anything	**3** something
(g)	**1** proud	**2** happy	**3** angry
(h)	**1** for	**2** against	**3** after

2 Write a short paragraph about a competition you entered.

What was the competition?
How did you feel?
Who won?

3 Write the correct form of *have to* or *don't have to*.

a) Caroline .... win the competition to keep Applewind.
b) Caroline's dad says she .... learn that life is about winning.
c) Caroline .... tell Mr Morley what Fred did.
d) Luckily, they .... call the police.
e) Caroline .... leave the stables.
f) Fred .... muck out the stables.

4 Who says the sentences below? Write their names below the speech bubbles.

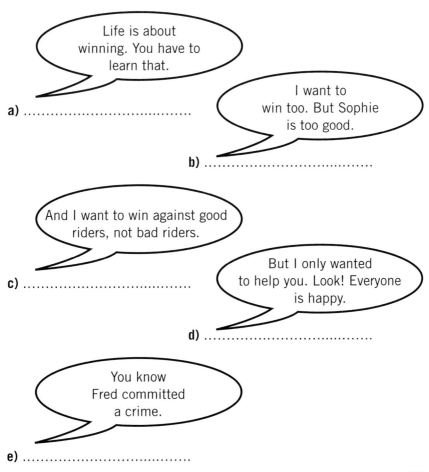

Life is about winning. You have to learn that.

a) ....

I want to win too. But Sophie is too good.

b) ....

And I want to win against good riders, not bad riders.

c) ....

But I only wanted to help you. Look! Everyone is happy.

d) ....

You know Fred committed a crime.

e) ....

After Reading

1 **Harriet Jones is seventeen. She works as a stable hand on Cherry Tree Farm. You are going to listen to her talking about her job. First answer the questions as a class.**

   a) Would you like to be a stable hand? Why/Why not?
   b) What do you think would be the most difficult thing about the job?

2 **Now listen and complete the summary of Harriet's typical day.**

Harriet's Day

   a) I .... at 6 am.
   b) I'm in the...............by 7.15 am.
   c) I feed...............with hay.
   d) I take the horses out to................
   e) I .... the stables.
   f) I .... the horses.
   g) I...............their bridles and saddles.
   h) I finish at.........
   i) Then I...............my own horse Hector. Fantastic!

3 **Does Harriet like her job? What does she like about it? What does she not like about?**

4 **Find out about a job you would like to do. Write a short paragraph about it. Then tell a friend.**

Quiz Time

5 What do you know about horses? Do our quiz and find out.

1 Do horses grow out of their shoes?
a) ☐ Yes
b) ☐ No

2 How long do horses live for?
a) ☐ 10 to 15 years
b) ☐ 20 to 25 years

3 Do horses sleep lying down?
a) ☐ Yes
b) ☐ No

4 How much time do horses spend eating grass every day?
a) ☐ 11 to 13 hours
b) ☐ 5 to 10 hours

5 Can horses swim?
a) ☐ Yes
b) ☐ No

6 Now listen and check your answers.

7 In pairs write a quiz about your favourite animal. Then try your quiz out on some friends.

After Reading

Puzzle

1 Read the clues and complete the puzzle with words from the story.

a) Horses live here.
b) Stable hands do this every day to keep the stables clean.
c) If you win a show jumping competition, you get one of these.
d) When you win a race, a match or a competition you are called this.
e) People who like horses join these.
f) Horses jump over these in competitions.

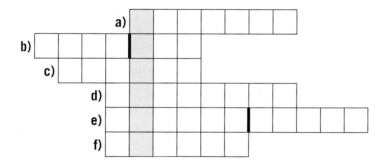

2 What do the letters in the green squares spell? Write three sentences about the person.

a) ....

b) ....

c) ....